This is the first edition of The Little Person Inside.
Printed in England, 2021. Published by NISCHNASCH.
Written by Talan Skeels-Piggins. Illustrated, coedited and designed by Natascha Taylor. The author and illustrator assert the moral right to be identified as the creators of the work. All rights reserved. No part of this publication may be reproduced, stored in a retrieval system, or transmitted in any form or by any means electronic, mechanical, photocopying, recording or otherwise, without prior permission of NISCHNASCH.
London, United Kingdom. ISBN 978-1-912206-32-2
www.nischnasch.com / info@nischnasch.com

"This book is dedicated to all those who supported me and believed in me."

Talan Skeels-Piggins

©nischnasch

Talan loved to play outside.
He learned to ride his purple bicycle.

...and jumped sky HIGH on trampolines!

He was always **happy** to teach others how to play. And so, he joined a **big school** and became the **PE Teacher!**

But not all days can be happy,
and some days are **very** hard.
One day, on his way to play sport with
his friends, Talan was in a **bad** accident.
The Doctors and Nurses had to **work very
hard to help him.**

THIS WAS AN

EMERGENCY!

They worked all day and all night,
they did their very best,
and Talan's life was **saved!**

However, Talan's back was hurt so badly
that he could no longer move his legs,
he would never walk again.
This felt impossible.

Talan was very sad.
He thought he would never play again.
This made Talan cry.

The world felt very dark around him,
and he felt scared.
"How can I live without my legs?"
he thought. Even though Talan was
a teacher, he felt lost.

Sometimes we all feel lost.

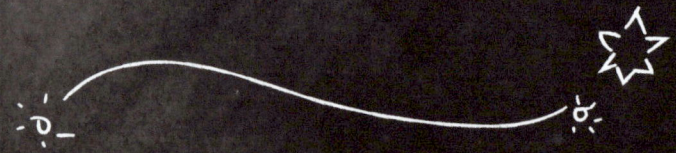

"Why not try skiing?"

Talan thought the man was making it up, after all, **how could someone who cannot use their legs go skiing?**

The man explained that you can ski using a special seat, with arm sticks and some skis. **It really is possible** for someone who is 'sat-down' to go skiing!

Talan was worried, he didn't understand. Then **the little person inside his heart** spoke up and Talan **listened**. This little person is inside each of us. He was reminded that **he can do ANYTHING. That he must BELIEVE in himself!**

The day felt warmer, **the sun began to shine.**

Talan thought the idea was amazing, he remembered that when he was younger he would ski with his family and it made him happy. "Maybe I will learn to ski" said Talan, "Maybe it will make me HAPPY again? I know, I will try to be the best skier I can be and go to the Winter Paralympics."

Talan's dream was huge! The Paralympics brings the **strongest** athletes together FROM ALL OVER THE WORLD.

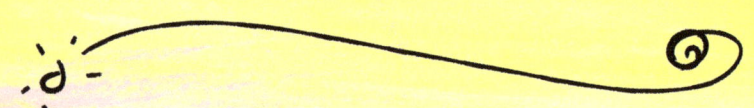

Talan began **the climb** towards his **dream.** He worked so hard. He grew **stronger** every **day.** He learned to use a **wheelchair.** He learned how to get in and out of his chair **using only** his arms. He learned **how to live** on his own all over again so that he could **leave the hospital.**

He worked **harder and harder** so he could **begin his adventure** to become a **sitting-down ski** racer for **Great Britain**.

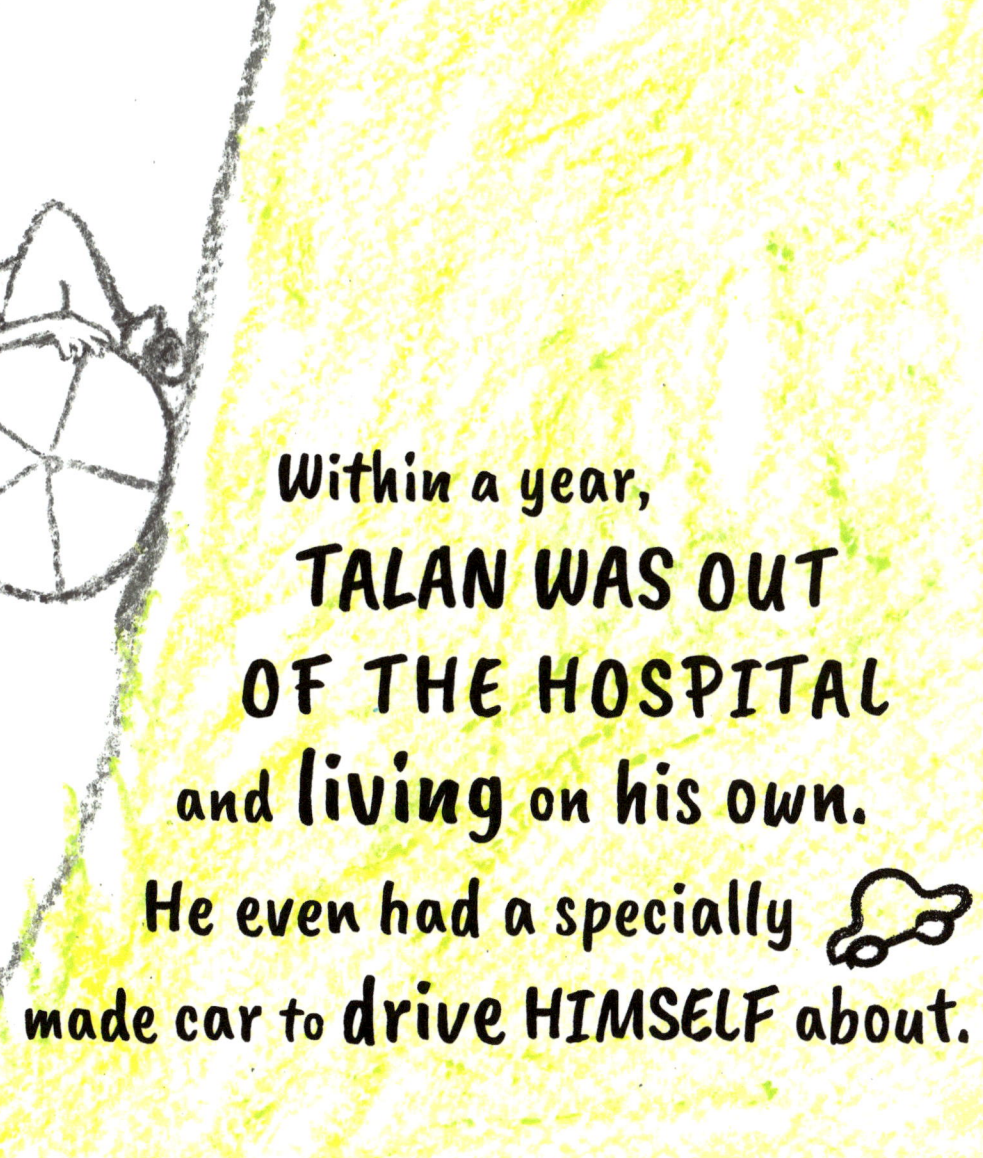

Within a year, **TALAN WAS OUT OF THE HOSPITAL** and **living** on his own. He even had a specially made car to **drive HIMSELF** about.

He was off on a trip to America!

He was going to Winter Park
to learn to sit-ski.

Talan had never been so **nervous** in his life.

Lots of people had told him he was silly to try to sit-ski,

because he had no use of his legs or his tummy

muscles to help him balance.

For the first five days of the trip, poor Talan fell over non-stop. He could not move more than five yards before falling over into the snow. Five yards is only a bit longer than a car.

"Give up" said the instructors. "Give up, you are the worst pupil we have ever seen, all you do is fall over." Talan remembered the Little Person Inside and SPOKE UP.

"I am going to be a ski racer," said Talan "I am going to give it one more go."

On the very next day, Talan managed to stop falling over as much. One time he managed to ski from the top of the mountain to the bottom without going 'splat' into the snow. By going one more time, **BY NOT GIVING UP,** he had his breakthrough and had begun to actually ski.

After a few more trips to the mountains, Talan had improved his skiing. He changed the sit-ski to include shoulder straps, so that by shrugging his shoulders he could control the ski and turn left and right.

He still managed to **fall over a lot**, and sometimes would **get stuck** on the ski lifts.

Clive, who was helping Talan, had to try and lift him down. They would often end up in a big pile.

Talan wanted to get better at skiing, and the best way to learn is from the experts. Experts are people who are especially good at what they do. He learned that the British Disabled Ski Team would be in France for training and finding new team members.

He went with Clive to the mountains again.

He watched. He learned.
He did better!

He was becoming so good he was invited to join the Development Squad of the British Team. This brought Talan even closer to his dream!

Talan trained on snow for the winters. In the summers he trained in the gym. He never gave up. Talan became a ski racer just as he dreamed!

He became a member of the BRITISH 'A' TEAM!

He competed in Europe, in America, in New Zealand and even in South Korea. He still had lots of crashes though, it wasn't an easy journey.

The Little Person Inside continued to remind him, **"WHEN TIMES ARE TOUGH YOU MUST KEEP GOING"**. Finally, Talan became part of **the Team Great Britain** going to the 2010 Winter Paralympics.

He was determined to win the Gold Medal and prove to everyone that he could **really be the best racer in the World**. He was skiing really well and felt that it was **his moment to shine**.

The race was **very icy**.
This was very hard for Talan.

He went as fast as he possibly could, and he managed 15th place!

There was no gold medal for 15th place though and without the gold Talan felt he had failed. He felt he had let down all his friends, his family and his country.

He returned to his room in the Athletes Village and he hid from everyone.
He felt useless.

The coach came and spoke with Talan. They talked about the race. He told the coach that he had raced as fast as he possibly could, he had given everything. The coach said "I am proud of you. Giving your best is the most important thing in life."

Talan then realised he could not have done any better, and so he became pleased with his best effort, because if you are THE BEST YOU CAN BE, you are your own CHAMPION.

Nine months later, Talan took part in the next set of skiing races. The same people, who had beaten him last time, were there. This included the World and Paralympic Champions. The snow was very soft for the race. Talan gave the race his very best effort again and ended up with the Gold medal this time.

Talan says "Remember, so long as you are always THE BEST YOU CAN BE, you can be proud of yourself. Everyone will see that YOU ARE A CHAMPION!"

This is a TRUE story.

Talan would not change his life. He would not choose to turn back time and have his legs back. After talking with his Little Person Inside, he realised that he has been ABLE to help more people now than he would have done if he hadn't been in the accident. HIS LIFE HAS MORE MEANING and he is PROUD to be in a wheelchair.

Talan has also become a **famous motorcycle racer** and double world champion....

but that is for another story.